AUTHENTIC CHORDS
ORIGINAL KEYS
COMPLETE SONGS

The JOHN HIATT COLLECTION

T0045055

Arranged by Jeff Schofield

ISBN 978-0-634-03269-1

HAL•LEONARD® CORPORATION

7777 W. BLUEMOUND RD. P.O. BOX 13819 MILWAUKEE, WI 53213

Visit Hal Leonard Online at
www.halleonard.com

The JOHN HIATT COLLECTION

CONTENTS

HOW TO USE THIS BOOK

Strum It is the series designed especially to get you playing (and singing!) along with your favorite songs. The idea is simple—the songs are arranged using their original keys in lead sheet format, giving you the chords for each song, beginning to end. The melody and lyrics are also shown to help you keep your spot and sing along.

Rhythm slashes are written above the staff as an accompaniment suggestion. Strum the chords in the rhythm indicated. Use the chord diagrams found at the top of the first page of the arrangement for the appropriate chord voicings.

Additional Musical Definitions

⊓	• Downstroke
v	• Upstroke
D.S. al Coda	• Go back to the sign (𝄋), then play until the measure marked *"To Coda,"* then skip to the section labelled *"Coda."*
D.C. al Fine	• Go back to the beginning of the song and play until the measure marked *"Fine"* (end).
cont. rhy. sim.	• Continue using similar rhythm pattern.
N.C.	• Instrument is silent (drops out).
𝄆 𝄇	• Repeat measures between signs.
1. 2.	• When a repeated section has different endings, play the first ending only the first time and the second ending only the second time.

Drive South

Words and Music by John Hiatt

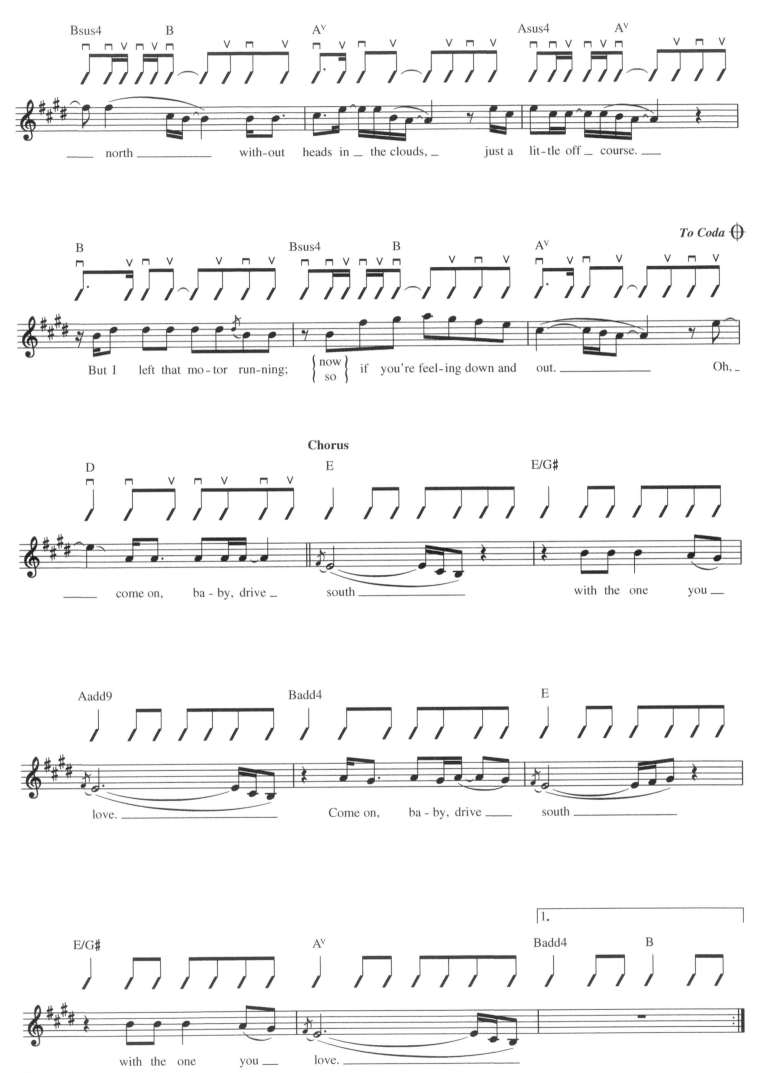

Bridge

Spoken: And I heard your mama callin',   I think she was just stallin'.

Don't know who she was talkin' to.   Ba - by, me and you.   We could go down with a smile _ on.

Don't both - er to pack _ your ny - lons,   just leave those pret - ty legs show-in';   it gets _ hot down where we're

Interlude

go - in'.   Bet - ter be - lieve it,   ba - by.   Hey, _____

hee. _____

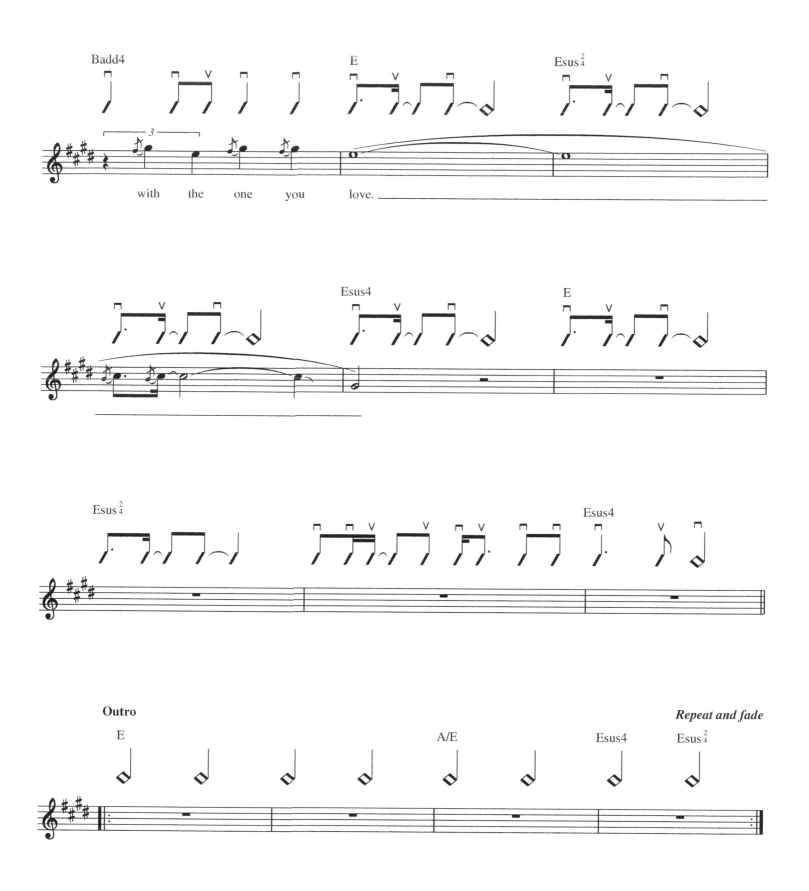

Additional Lyrics

2. I'm not talkin' 'bout retreatin', little girl,
   Gonna take our stand in this Chevy van.
   Windows open on the rest of the world,
   Holdin' hands all the way to Dixieland.

Pre-Chorus 2. We've been try'n' to turn our lives around
   Since we were little kids,
   It's been wearin' us down.
   Don't turn away now, darlin',
   Let's fire it up and wind it out.
   Oh, come on, baby, drive south...

Angel Eyes

Words and Music by John Hiatt and Fred Koller

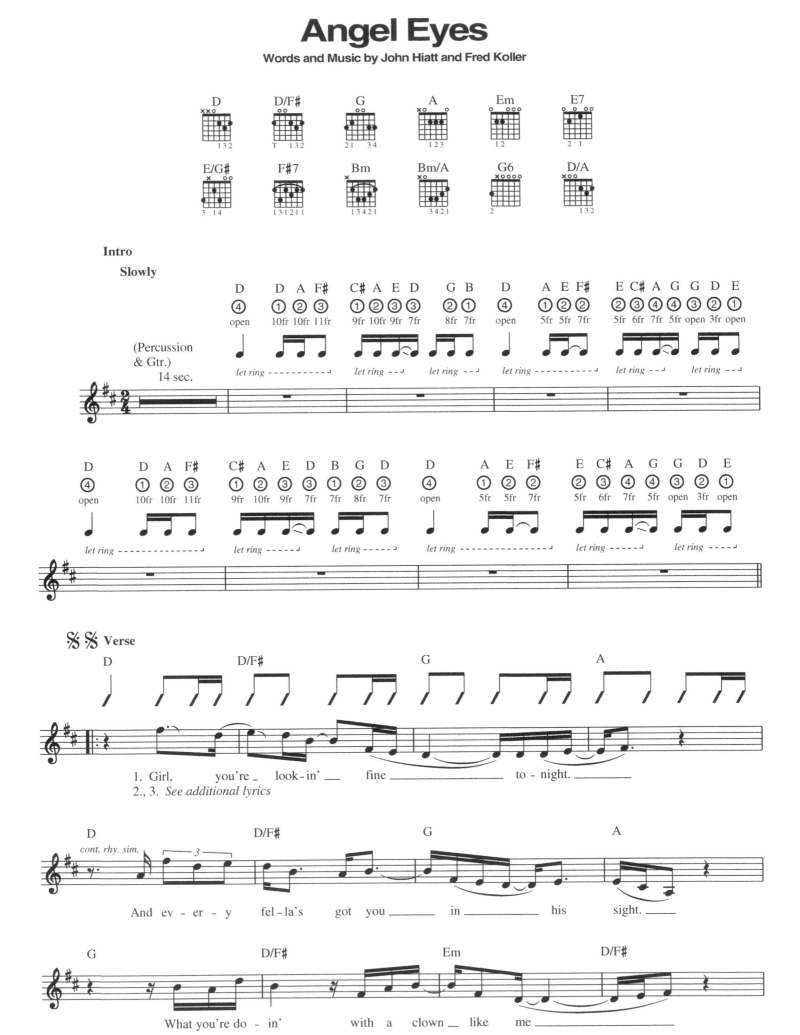

is sure - ly one of life's __ lit - tle mys - ter - ies. _____ So to -

𝄋 **Chorus**

night _____ I'll ask _____ the stars __ a - bove, _____

3rd time, Instrumental

how did I _____ ev - er win _____ your _____ love. _____

What did I do, what _ did I say

1.

To Coda 1 ⊕
To Coda 2 ⊕

let ring - - - - - - - - - - -

to turn ___ your ___ an - gel ___ eyes _ my way? _____

2.

let ring - - - - 」 let ring - - - - 」 let ring - - - - - - - - - - - - - 」 let ring - - - - 」 let ring - - - - 」

eyes _ my way. ___

11

Bridge

Don't an-y-one ___ wake ___ me ___ if this is a dream,

be-cause she's the best ___ thing ___ that's ev - er hap - pened to me. ___

___ All you fel - las, ___ yeah, you can look all ___ you like. ___

___ But this girl you see ___ she's a leav-in' here ___ with a me ___ to - night. ___

D.S. al Coda 1

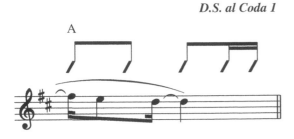

$\bigoplus$ **Coda 1**   *D.S.S. al Coda 2*

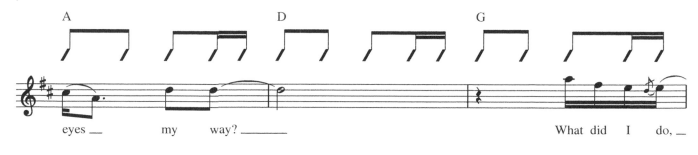

eyes __ my way? _____ What did I do, __

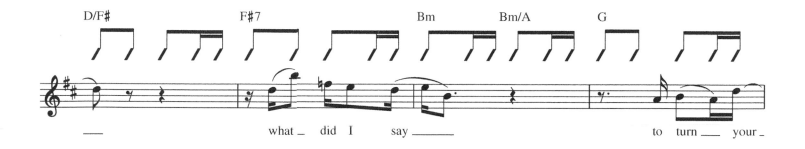

__ what _ did I say _____ to turn __ your _

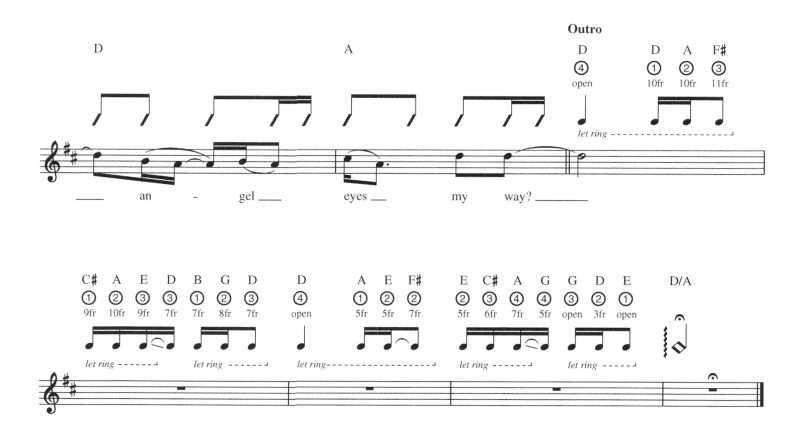

__ an - gel __ eyes __ my way? _____

Additional Lyrics

2. And I'm the guy who never learned to dance.
   I never even got one second glance.
   Across a crowded room, well, that was close enough.
   Well, I could look but I could never touch.

3. And there's just one more thing I need to know:
   If this is love, why does it scare me so?
   (There) must be somethin' only you can see,
   But, girl, I feel it when you look at me.

Buffalo River Home

Words and Music by John Hiatt

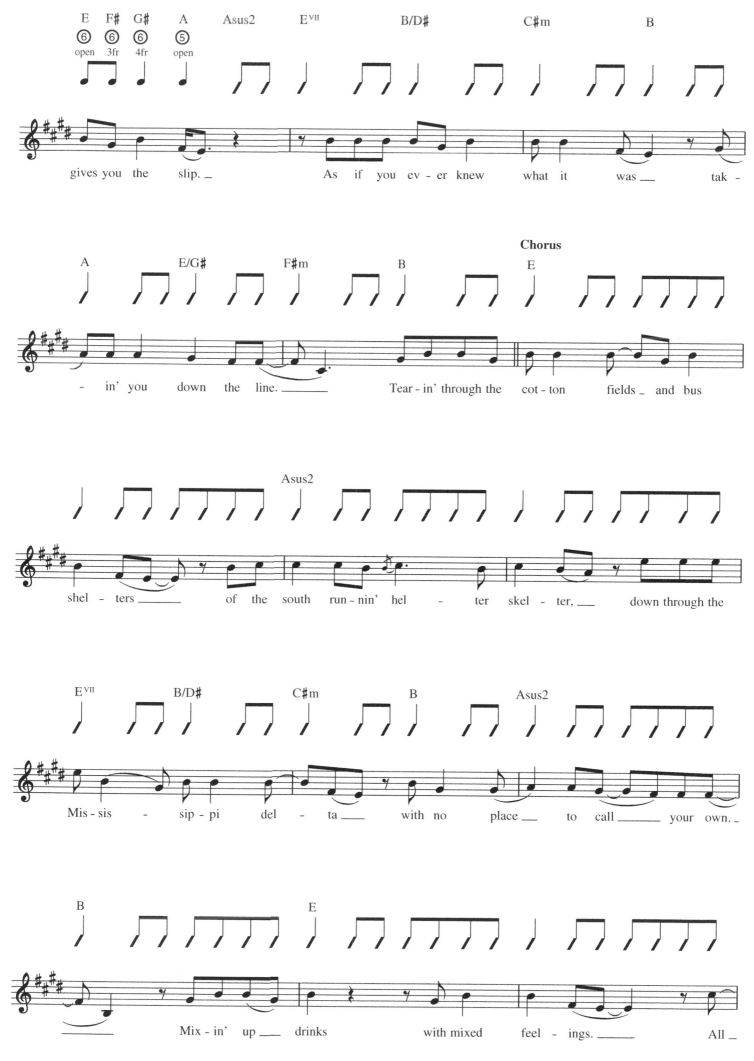

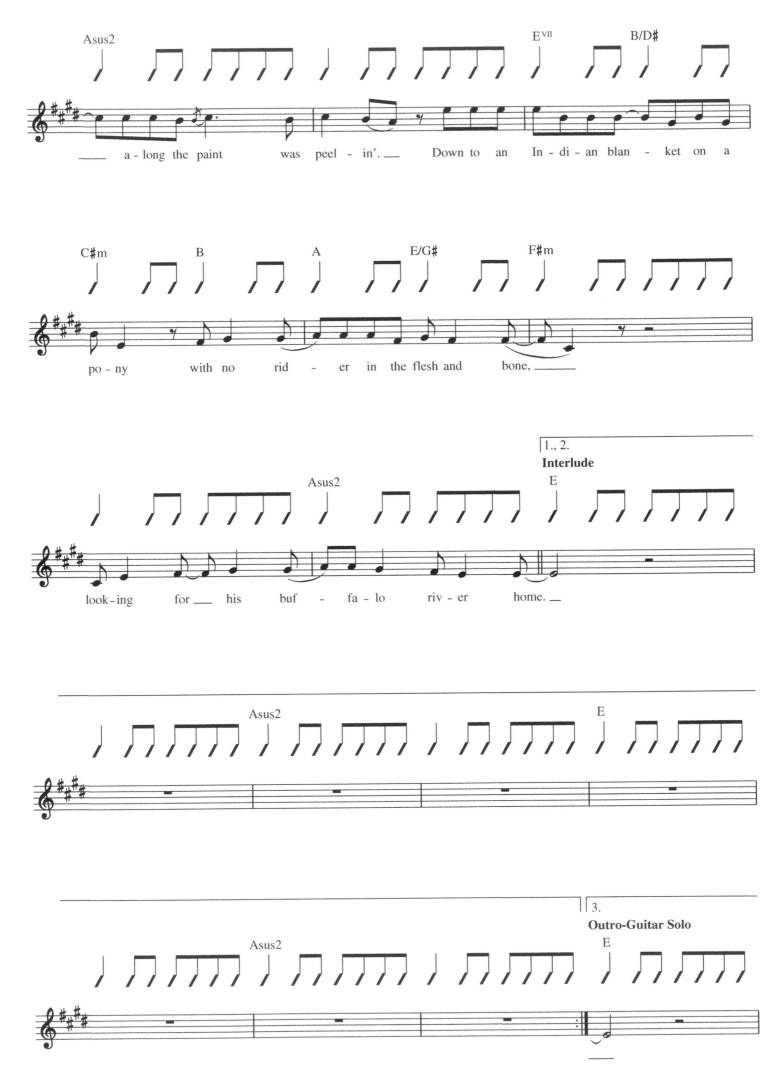

Additional Lyrics

2. I've been circling the wagons
   Down at Times Square,
   Trying to fill up this hole in my soul
   But nothing fits there.
   Just when you think you can let it rip
   You're pounding the pavement in your daddy's wingtips.
   As if you had someplace else to go
   Or a better way to get there.

3. Now there's only two things in life,
   But I forget what they are.
   It seems we're either hangin' on a moonbeam's coattails
   Or wishing on stars.
   Just when you think that you've been gypped
   The bearded lady comes and does a double back flip,
   And you run off and join the circus.
   Yeah, you just let that pony ride.

Child of the Wild Blue Yonder

Words and Music by John Hiatt

wom - an raised _ her.   The spir - it fa - ther praised _ her. ___

Thru their love ___ she was ___ set free, ___

hee, hee. ___   From a ba - by kick - in' and scream - in'

to a full - blood - ed wom - an, ___ dream - in' ___ with the pow -

- er just ___ to be. ___

Guitar Solo

* Sing 1st time

She's a

Additional Lyrics

3. And if you see her fallin',
   That's just a little trick she does. Mm-hh.
   She makes a dive for the pain that's callin',
   Then heads for the clouds like a little dove.

4. She can't help her laughin';
   And she can't stop your cryin' days,
   Sometimes it hurts to be havin',
   To hold onto a love that surely must fly away.

Cry Love

Words and Music by John Hiatt

bone. _____

Verse

do _____ when the plan-ets shift? _ A what you gon-na do? _____ Gon-na slit your _

4. *See additional lyrics*

wrists, _ and bleed all o - ver the Milk-y ___ Way. _ The stars in your

Chorus

eyes _____ look red to - day. _ Cry love, cry

love. _ The tears of an an - gel, _____ the tears of a dove. _ A spill-ing all o -

To Coda

- ver, _____ your heart from a - bove. _____ Cry love, cry

love. _____

2. Now what you gon-na

3. The trust of a

Additional Lyrics

4. Throwing up ashes on the floor.
   If this is a lesson in love, well, what's it for?
   The heart won't remember the burning fire,
   The next time you feel the flame of desire.

Feels Like Rain

Words and Music by John Hiatt

Outro

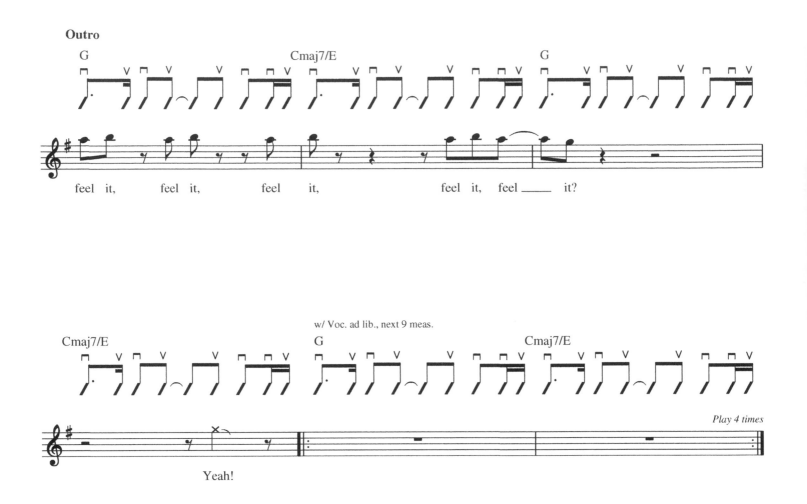

feel it,   feel it,   feel   it,   feel it, feel _____ it?

Yeah!

Play 4 times

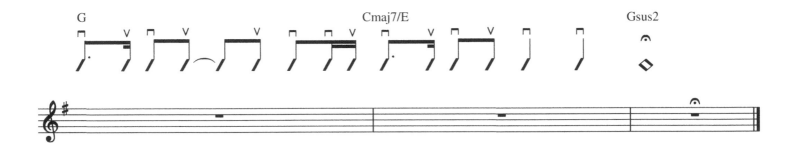

Additional Lyrics

2. Lyin' underneath the stars, right next to you
   I'm wonderin' who you are, and how do you do?
   How do you do, baby?
   (When) the clouds blow in across the moon,
   And the wind howls out your name.
   And it feels like rain.
   And it feels like rain.
Spoken: Baby, can you feel it?

4. So batten down the hatches, baby,
   But leave your heart out on your sleeve.
   It looks like we're in for stormy weather, but
   That ain't no cause for us to leave.
   Just lie here in my arms
   And let it wash away the pain.
   And it feels like rain.
   And it feels like rain.

Have a Little Faith in Me

Words and Music by John Hiatt

faith in __ me. _____

Have a lit-tle faith in __ me, _____

well, have a lit-tle faith in __ me. _____

Verse

3. 'Cause I've been lov-ing you

for such a long __ time, __ ba - by, ex-pect-in' noth-in' in re-turn. Just for you to have

a lit-tle faith _ in me. _ You see, time, _____ time is __ our friend. _

'Cause for us there is __ no end. _____ All we got-ta do is have a lit-tle

30

Additional Lyrics

2. And when your secret heart
   Cannot speak so easily,
   Come here, darlin', from a whisper start.
   To have a little faith in me.
   And when your back's against the wall
   Just turn around and a you will see
   That I'll be there, I'll be there to catch your fall.
   So have a little faith in me.

Lipstick Sunset

Words and Music by John Hiatt

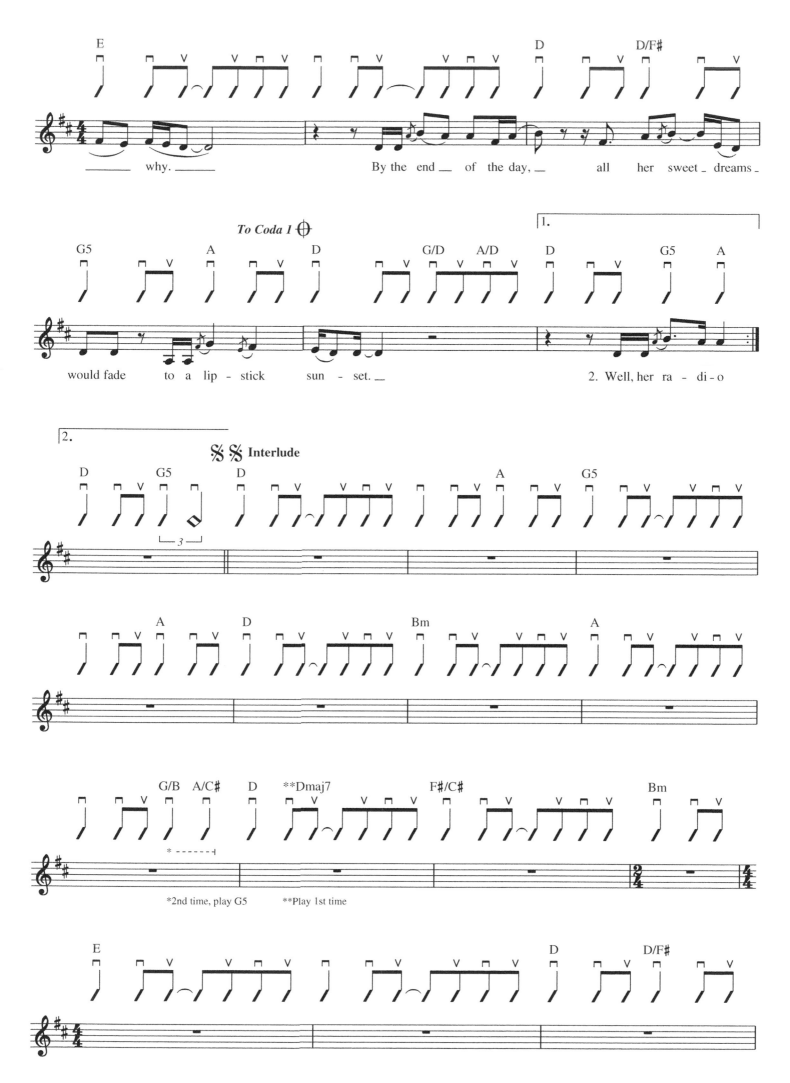

_____ why. _____   By the end _ of the day, _   all   her   sweet _ dreams _

To Coda 1 ⊕

would fade   to   a   lip - stick   sun - set. _   2. Well, her ra - di - o

2.

𝄋 𝄋 **Interlude**

└─ 3 ─┘

*2nd time, play G5   **Play 1st time

Additional Lyrics

2. Well, her radio was playin',
   And that ol' summer heat was on the rise,
   I just had to get away
   Before some sad old song
   Brought more tears to my eyes.
   And Lord, I couldn't tell her
   That her love was only killin' me.
   Oh, by the dawnin' of the day,
   All her sweet dreams would fade
   To a lipstick sunset.

3. Well, it's pretty as a picture, baby.
   Red and blushin' just before the night.
   Mm, maybe love's like that for me.
   Maybe I can only see
   As you take away the light.
   But hold me in the darkness;
   We can dream about the cool twilight,
   'Til the dawnin' of the day,
   When I will make my getaway
   To a lipstick sunset.

Memphis in the Meantime

Words and Music by John Hiatt

don't get out ___ of here ___ pret-ty soon ___ my head's ___ go-ing to ex - plode. ___

___ Sure, I like coun-try mu - sic and

To Coda ⊕

I like man-do-lins, ___ but right now I need a Tel - e-cast-

- er through a Vib - ro-Lux ___ turned up to ten. ___

Let's go to Mem -

Chorus

- phis in ___ the mean - time, ba - by.

36

Let's go to
Mem - phis in ___ the mean - time, ___ girl. ___

1.
___

2.
Let's go to Mem -

- phis in ___ the mean - time, ba - by.

Let's go to Mem - phis in ___ the mean - time, ___ girl. ___

Bridge
A7
May - be there's

A7sus$\frac{4}{6}$
A7(no3rd)
A7sus$\frac{4}{6}$
noth - in' hap - pen - in' there, ___ but may - be there's some - thin' in ___ the air, ___

hey.

(But) be - fore our up - per lips __ get

stiff, may - be we need __ us a big old whiff. __

D.S. al Coda   Coda

3. If we could

Cad - il - lac __ and change the

mes - sage on the Code - a - phone. __

Outro

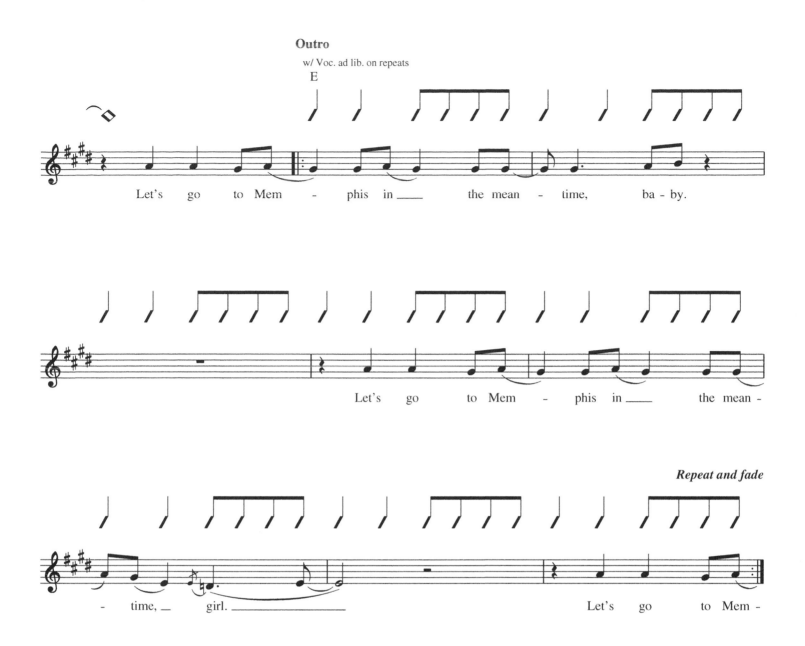

Additional Lyrics

2. I need a little shot of that rhythm, baby,
   Mixed up with these country blues.
   I wanna trade in these ol' cowboy boots
   For some fine Italian shoes.
   Forget the mousse and the hair spray, sugar,
   We don't need none of that.
   Naw, a little dab'll do ya, girl,
   Underneath a pork pie hat.
   Until hell freezes over,
   Well, maybe you can't wait that long.
   But I don't think Ronnie Milsap's
   Gonna ever record this song.

3. If we could just get off a that beat, little girl,
   Maybe we could find the groove.
   At least we can get ourselves a decent meal
   Down at The Rendezvous.
   'Cause one more heart-felt steel guitar chord,
   Girl, it's gonna do me in.
   I need to hear some trumpet and saxophone,
   You know, sounds as sweet as sin.
   And after we get good and greasy,
   Baby, we can come on home.
   But the cowhorns back on the Cadillac
   And change the message on the Code-a-phone.

Perfectly Good Guitar

Words and Music by John Hiatt

D.S. al Coda 2

4. There

✛ **Coda 2**

Verse

5. Late   at   night,   the   end   of   the   road.   He   wish – es   he   still   had   that

old   gui – tar   to   hold. ___   He'd   rock   it   like ___   a   ba – by   in   his   arms; ___

Chorus

nev – er   let   it   come ___   to   an – y   harm.   Oh,   it   breaks   my   heart   to

Additional Lyrics

2. It started back in 1963.
His momma wouldn't buy him that new red Harmony.
He settled for a sunburst with a crack,
But he's still tryin' to break his momma's back.
Oh, it breaks my heart...

3. Well, he loved that guitar just like a girlfriend.
But ev'ry good thing comes to an end.
Now he just sits in his room all day,
Whistlin' ev'ry note he ever played.

4. There oughta be a law with no bail,
Smash a guitar and you go to jail.
With no chance for early parole,
Ya don't get out until you get some soul.
Oh, it breaks my heart...

A Real Fine Love

Words and Music by John Hiatt

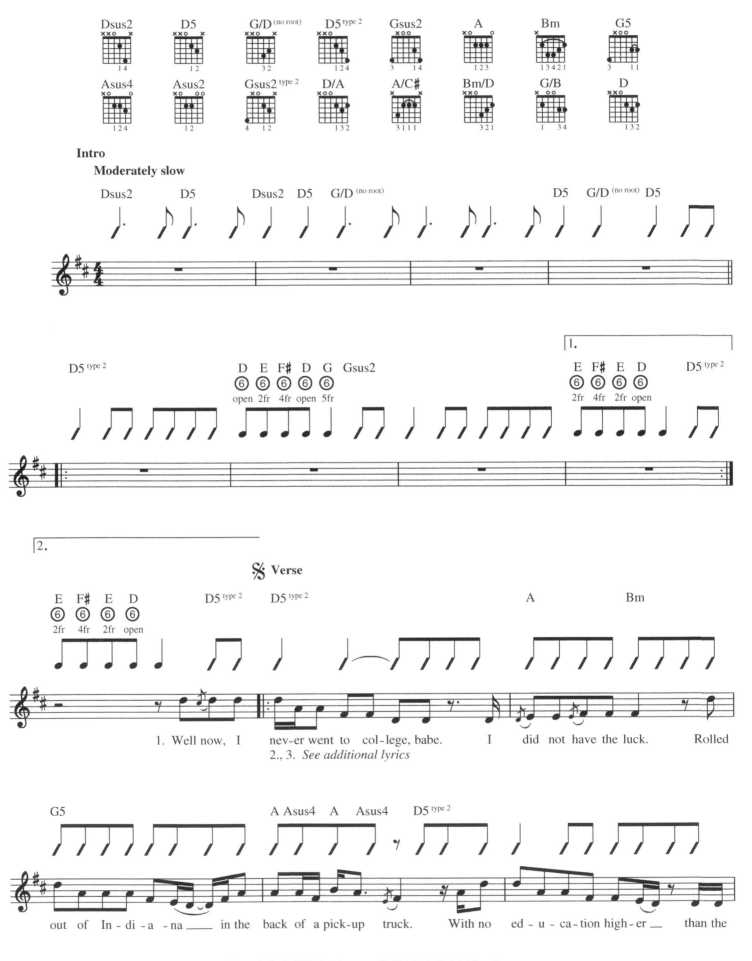

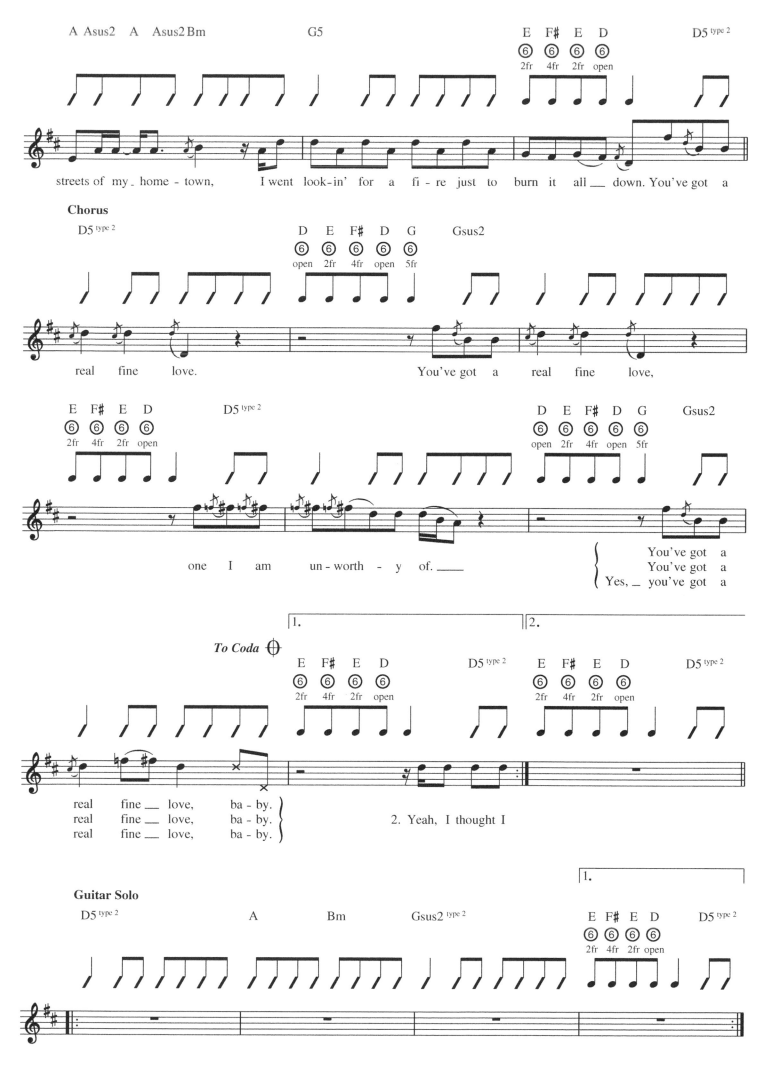

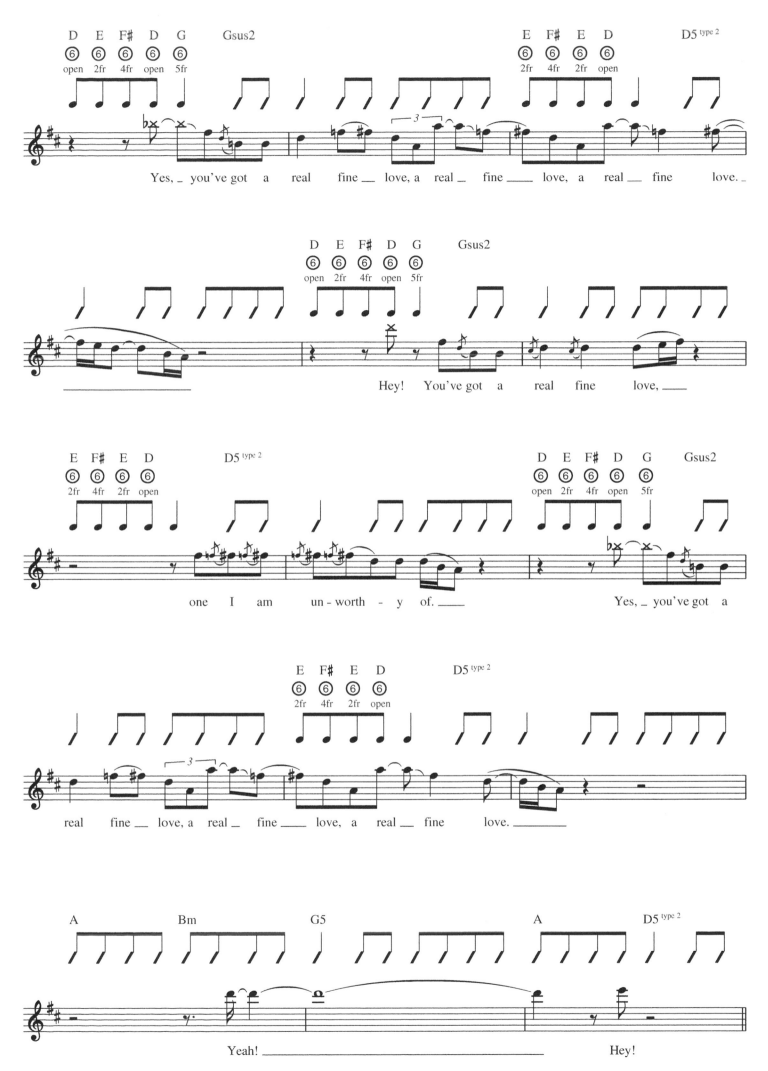

Outro

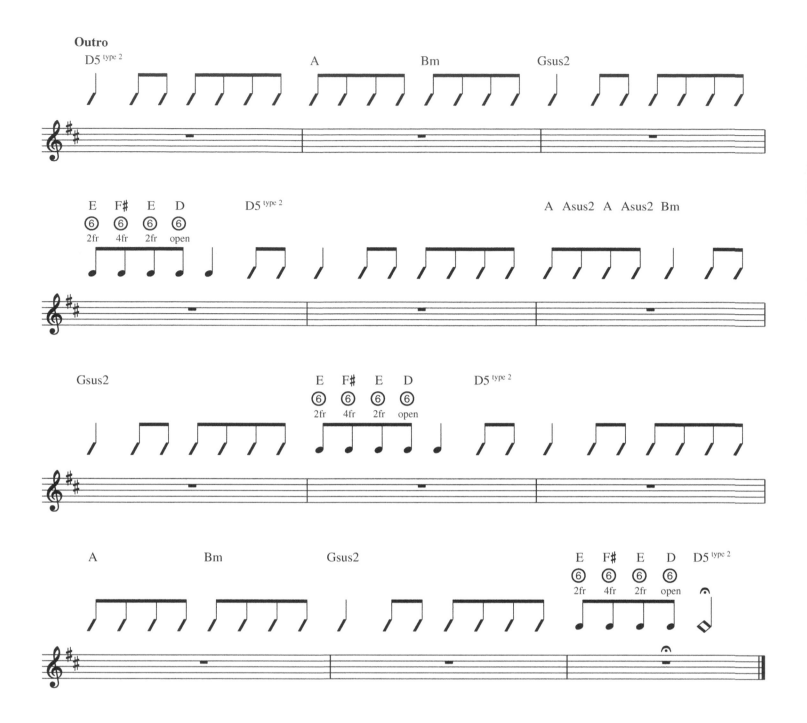

Additional Lyrics

2. Yeah, I thought I had a line on something
   Maybe no one else could say.
   And they couldn't find it in their hearts
   To just get out of my way.
   Then out of nowhere, and for nothin',
   You came into my life.
   I'd seen an angel or two before,
   But I never asked one to be my wife.

3. Well, you can sprinkle all your teardrops
   Across the evenin' sky,
   But you cannot hide the twinkle
   Of starlight in your eye.
   Well, I left my map way back there, baby.
   I don't know where we are.
   But I'm gonna pull my pony up
   And hitch my wagon to your star.

Slow Turning

Words and Music by John Hiatt

Additional Lyrics

2. Now I'm in my car,
   Ooh, I got the radio on.
   And now I'm a-yellin' at the kids in the back
   'Cause they're bangin' like Charlie Watts.
   You think you've come so far, huh,
   In this one-horse town;
   Then she's laughin' that crazy laugh
   'Cause you haven't left the parking lot.

Pre-Chorus Time is short, and here's the damn thing about it:
   You're gonna die, gonna die for sure.
   And you can learn to live with love or without it,
   But there ain't no cure.
   There's just a slow turning...

Riding With the King

Words and Music by John Hiatt

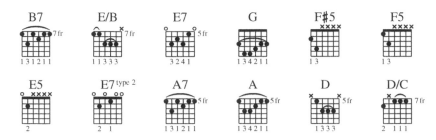

Intro

Moderate Blues

1. I dreamed I

Verse

did a good job and I got well paid, ___ blew it all at the
2. *See additional lyrics*

pen - ny ar - cade. ___

A hun-dred dol-lars on a Kew-pie doll; ___ I guess ___ no ___ white chick is gon-na

make __ me crawl. __   That's right.

Chorus

On a T. W. __ A. __ to the

See additional lyrics

prom-ised land, _____ ev - 'ry wom-an, child __ and man gets a,

a Cad - il - lac and a dia - mond ring. _____

Don't you know we're rid - in' with the king?

2. He's on a   We're rid - in' with the

53

king.

Bridge

A red cape and a shin-y Colt for-ty five, _____ hi – hive.

I nev-er saw his face, ___ but I ___ saw the light. _

_____ To-night ev-'ry-bod-y's

get-tin' their an – gel wings. _ D – don't you know we're rid-in' with the

Verse

cont. rhy. sim.

king? *Spoken: Well, I stepped out of mirror at ten years old, with a suit cut sharp as a razor and a*

heart full of gold. I had a guitar hangin' just about   waist high, and I'm gonna play that thing until the

Outro

day I die.

We're rid - in' with the   king, _____

ing, _____ ing. _____   Don't you know we're rid - in' with the

king? _____   We're rid - in' with the   king.

We're rid - in' with the...   Mm, _____

rid - in' with the   king. _   Mm. _____

Repeat and fade

Additional Lyrics

2. He's on a mission of mercy to the new frontier;
   He's gonna check us all on out of here.
   Up to that mansion on a hill
   Where you can get your prescription filled.
   Spoken: Any kind of pill.

Chorus Well, on a T.W.A. to the promised land,
   Ev'rybody come on, clap your hands.
   Don't you just love the way he sings?
   Don't you know we're ridin' with the king?
   We're ridin' with the king.

Tennessee Plates

Words and Music by John Hiatt and Mike Porter

woke up in a ho - tel, __ (and I) did - n't know what to do, I turned the T V on and wrote a

2., 3., 4. *See additional lyrics*

let - ter to you. __ The news was talk - in' 'bout a drag - net up on the in - ter -

To Coda 1

state;

said they were look-in' for a Cad-il-lac with

1.

Ten-nes-see plates.

2.

2. Well, since I Ten-nes-see plates. It was
See additional lyrics

Bridge

some-where in Ne-vad-a, cold out-side. __ She was shiv-'ring in the dark, so I

of-fered her a ride. Three bank jobs lat-er, four cars hot-wired, we

To Coda 2

crossed the Mis-sis-sip-pi, like an oil slick fi-re.

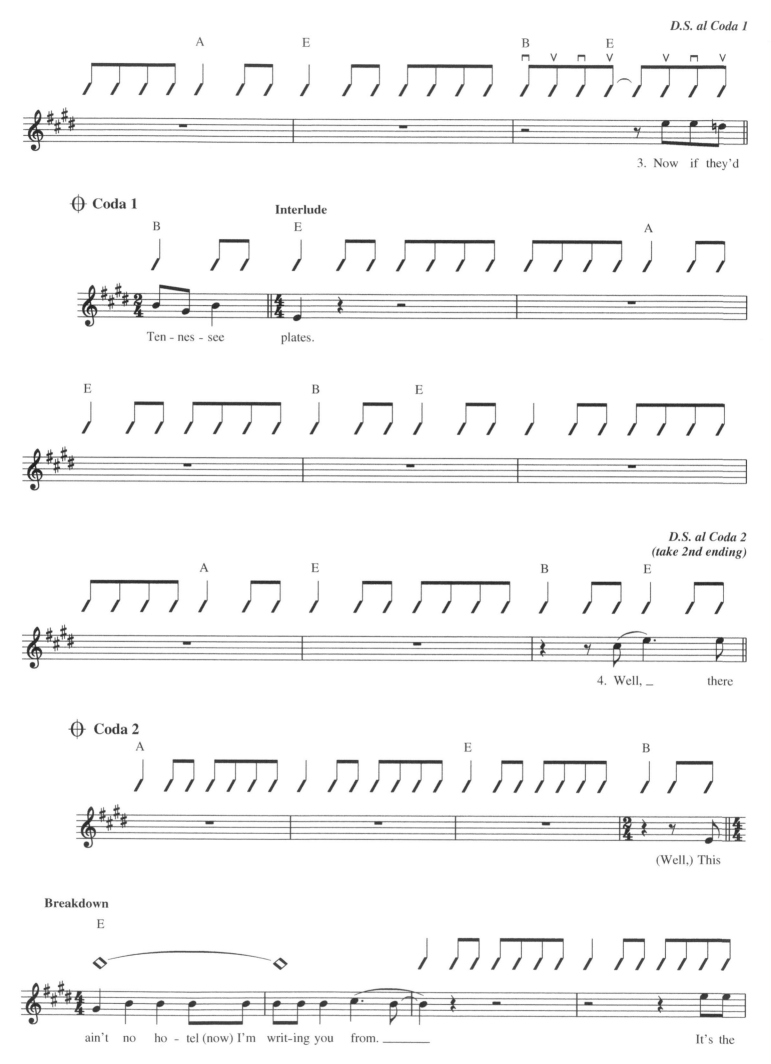

3. Now if they'd

⊕ Coda 1

Interlude

Ten - nes - see   plates.

D.S. al Coda 2
(take 2nd ending)

4. Well, __   there

⊕ Coda 2

(Well,) This

Breakdown

ain't   no   ho - tel (now) I'm writ-ing you   from. _____

It's the

Ten-nes-see pris-on up at Brush-y Moun - tain, _____ where yours sin-cere-ly's do-in' five __ to eight.

I'm just stamp-in' out my time mak-in' Ten-nes-see plates.

Outro

Additional Lyrics

2. Well, since I left California, baby, things have gotten worse;
It seems the land of opportunity for me is just a curse.
Tell that judge in Bakersfield, my trial-'ll have to wait;
Down here they're looking for a Cadillac with Tennessee plates.

3. Now if they'd known what we was up to, they wouldn't a let us in
When we landed in Memphis like original sin.
Up Elvis Presley Boulevard to the Graceland gates.
See, we were lookin' for a Cadillac with Tennessee plates.

4. Well, there must have been a dozen of 'em parked in that garage,
There wasn't one Lincoln and there wasn't one Dodge.
And there wasn't one Japanese model or make.
Just pretty, pretty Cadillacs with Tennessee plates.

Bridge She saw him singin' once when she was (only) seventeen,
And ever since that day she's been livin' in between.
I was never king of nothin' but this wild weekend.
Anyway, he wouldn't care; hell, he gave 'em to his friends.

Thing Called Love
(Are You Ready for This Thing Called Love)

Words and Music by John Hiatt

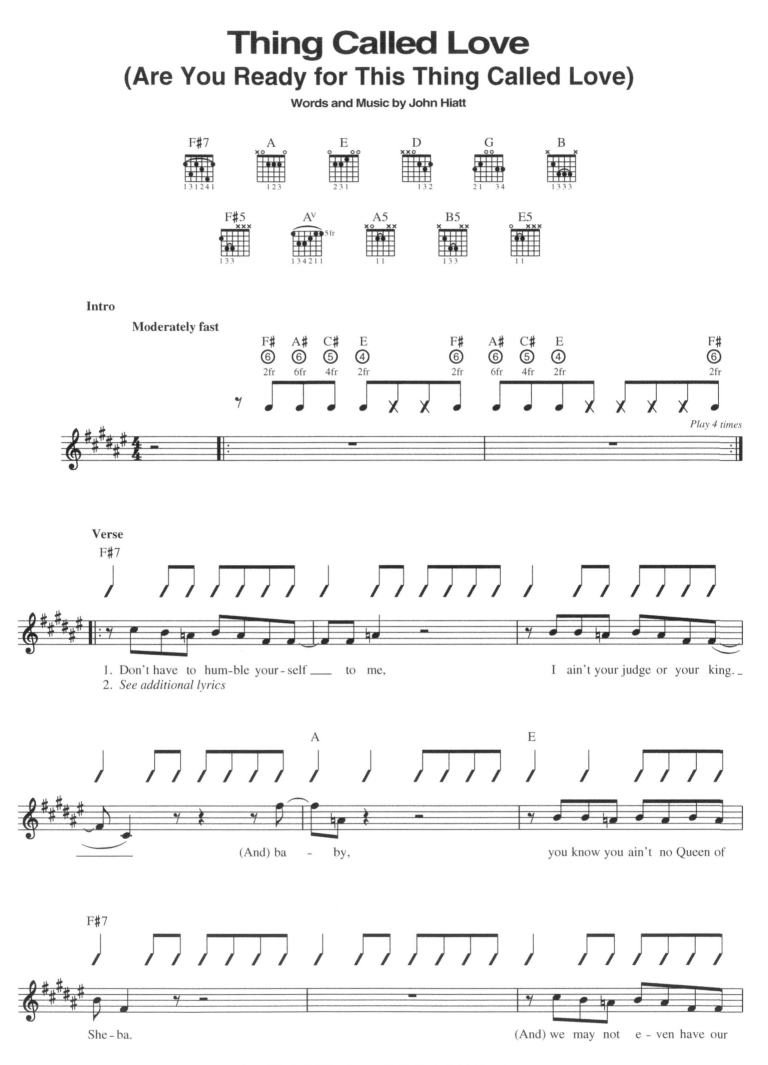

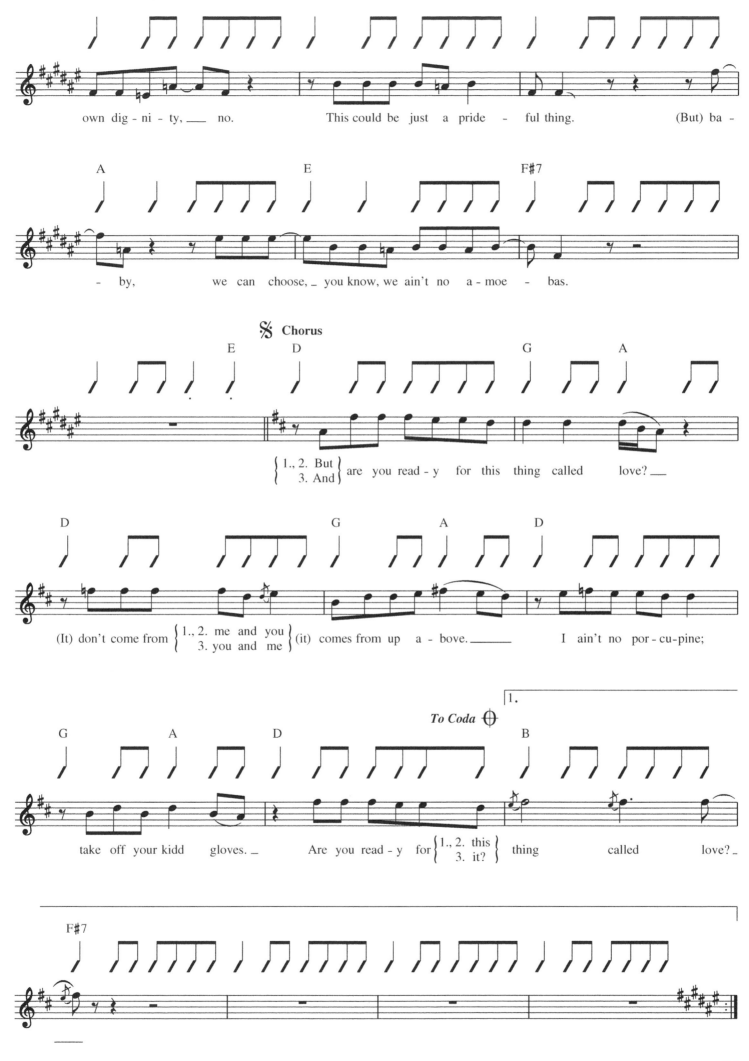

own dig - ni - ty, ___ no.   This could be just a pride - ful thing.   (But) ba -

A   E   F#7

- by,   we can choose, _ you know, we ain't no a - moe - bas.

𝄋 **Chorus**

E   D   G   A

{1., 2. But / 3. And} are you read - y   for   this   thing   called   love? ___

D   G   A   D

(It) don't come from {1., 2. me and you / 3. you and me} (it) comes from up a - bove. _____   I ain't no por - cu - pine;

1.

To Coda ⊕

G   A   D   B

take off your kidd gloves. _   Are you read - y for {1., 2. this / 3. it?} thing   called   love? _

F#7

Additional Lyrics

2. And you ain't some icon carved out of soap,
   Sent down here to clean up my reputation.
   (And) baby, I ain't your Prince Charming.
   Now we can live in fear, or act out of hope,
   For some kind of peaceful situation.
   Baby, don't know why the cry of love is so alarming.

The Way We Make a Broken Heart

Written by John Hiatt

Additional Lyrics

2. Lesson number one, we've just begun to hurt her so.
   And with lesson two she'll long for you when lights are low.
   And we get to lesson three when she gets down on her knees
   And begs you to stop at the door just before she comes apart.
   Oh, this is the way we make a broken heart.

3. And with lesson four there'll be no more for her to bear.
   And on some dark night we'll dim the lights on this affair.
   Then she'll find somebody new and he'll likely hurt her too.
   'Cause there must be millions just like you and me practiced in the art.

Through Your Hands

Words and Music by John Hiatt

2. *Male:* Still you

Verse

ar - gue for an op - tion. Still, you an - gle for __ your case __

3. *See additional lyrics*

__ like you would-n't __ know a burn - in' bush __ if it

blew up in __ your face. __ Yeah, *Both:* we scheme a - bout the fu-

- ture and we dream a - bout __ the past, __ when __

__ just __ a sim - ple reach - ing out __ might __ build __ a bridge that

Chorus

lasts. _ *Male:* And you ask, "What am I _____ not do - in'?" She says,
See additional lyrics

Female: "Your voice __ can - not com - mand. __ In ____ time ____ you will __ move

(Asus4)   (A7sus4)

moun - tains   *Both:* and it   will ___ come _____   through   your

(D)   (A/D)   (G/B^type 2)   (D)   (A/D)

hands." _

(G/B^type 2)   (D)   (A/D)   (G/B^type 2)

Male: Through   your _   hands. _

Guitar Solo

(D)   (A/D)   (G/B^type 2)   (Gsus2)

(D/F#)   (Em7)

D.S. al Coda

(Asus4)

3. *Male:* So, what -

Additional Lyrics

3. *Male:* So whatever your hands find to do
You must do with all your heart.
There are thoughts enough to blow men's minds
And tear great worlds apart.
There's a healin' touch to find you
On that broad highway somewhere,
Female: To lift you high as music flyin'
Through the angel's hair.

Chorus Both: Don't ask what you are not doin'
Male: Because your voice cannot command.
Both: In time we will move mountains.
And it will come through your hands.
Through your hands. Through your hands.

AUTHENTIC CHORDS • ORIGINAL KEYS • COMPLETE SONGS

The *Strum It* series lets players strum the chords and sing along with their favorite hits. Each song has been selected because it can be played with regular open chords, barre chords, or other moveable chord types. Guitarists can simply play the rhythm, or play and sing along through the entire song. All songs are shown in their original keys complete with chords, strum patterns, melody and lyrics. Wherever possible, the chord voicings from the recorded versions are notated.

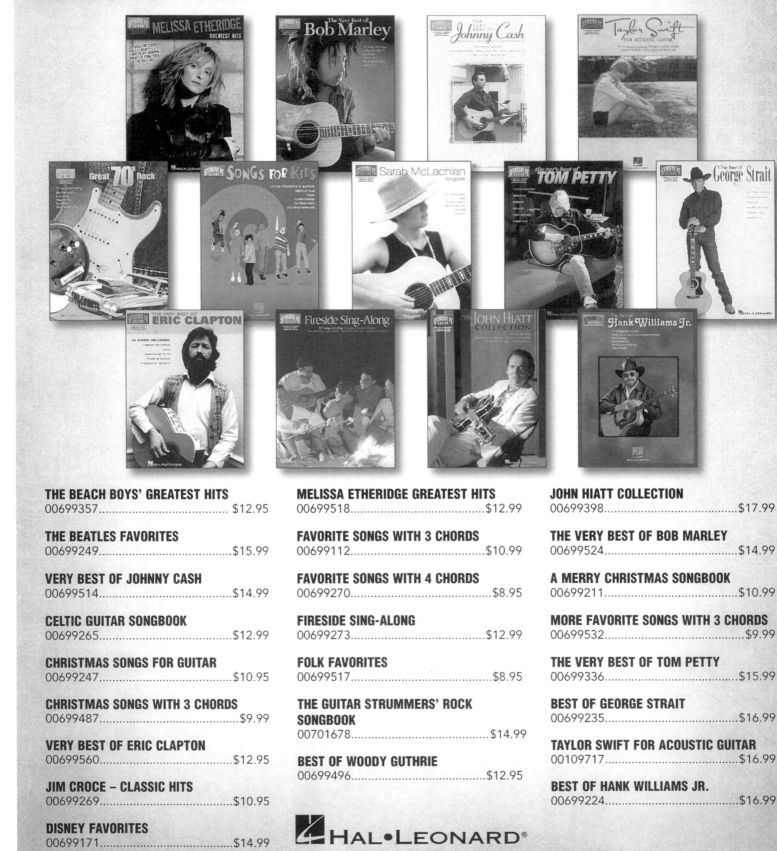

THE BEACH BOYS' GREATEST HITS
00699357.. $12.95

THE BEATLES FAVORITES
00699249.. $15.99

VERY BEST OF JOHNNY CASH
00699514.. $14.99

CELTIC GUITAR SONGBOOK
00699265.. $12.99

CHRISTMAS SONGS FOR GUITAR
00699247.. $10.95

CHRISTMAS SONGS WITH 3 CHORDS
00699487.. $9.99

VERY BEST OF ERIC CLAPTON
00699560.. $12.95

JIM CROCE – CLASSIC HITS
00699269.. $10.95

DISNEY FAVORITES
00699171.. $14.99

MELISSA ETHERIDGE GREATEST HITS
00699518.. $12.99

FAVORITE SONGS WITH 3 CHORDS
00699112.. $10.99

FAVORITE SONGS WITH 4 CHORDS
00699270.. $8.95

FIRESIDE SING-ALONG
00699273.. $12.99

FOLK FAVORITES
00699517.. $8.95

THE GUITAR STRUMMERS' ROCK SONGBOOK
00701678.. $14.99

BEST OF WOODY GUTHRIE
00699496.. $12.95

JOHN HIATT COLLECTION
00699398.. $17.99

THE VERY BEST OF BOB MARLEY
00699524.. $14.99

A MERRY CHRISTMAS SONGBOOK
00699211.. $10.99

MORE FAVORITE SONGS WITH 3 CHORDS
00699532.. $9.99

THE VERY BEST OF TOM PETTY
00699336.. $15.99

BEST OF GEORGE STRAIT
00699235.. $16.99

TAYLOR SWIFT FOR ACOUSTIC GUITAR
00109717.. $16.99

BEST OF HANK WILLIAMS JR.
00699224.. $16.99

HAL•LEONARD®

Visit Hal Leonard online at
www.halleonard.com